Tipping the Water Jar of Heaven

Poems by Sara Parrott

NINE MILE BOOKS

Publisher: Nine Mile Art Corp.
Editors: Bob Herz, Stephen Kuusisto, Andrea Scarpino
Art Editor Emeritus: Whitney Daniels
Cover Art: Andrew Parrott
Author photo: Philomena Leavitt

Nine Mile Books is an imprint of Nine Mile Art Corp.

The publishers gratefully acknowledge support of the New York State Council on the Arts with the support of Governor Andrew M. Cuomo and the New York State Legislature. We also acknowledge support of the County of Onondaga and CNY Arts through the Tier Three Project Support Grant Program. We have also received significant support from the Central New York Community Foundation. This publication would not have been possible without the generous support of these groups. We are very grateful to them all.

ISBN: 978-1-7354463-2-5

ACKNOWLEDGMENTS

Grateful appreciation is due the editors and staff of the following publications in which several poems in this collection first appeared:

Dappled Things
"Grasping the Hem of Divinity"

Ghost City Review
"Mother Daughter Smoke Rings"

Nine Mile Books & Literary Magazine
"In the Garden of You"

True Chili, Underwood Press
"Walking Through the Ramshackle Barn Dance"

The Literary Nest
"Shadowing the Farmer"

Special thanks to Steve Kuusisto and Bob Herz of Nine Mile Books & Magazine for shepherding this book; to staff and fellow writers at the Syracuse YMCA's Downtown Writers Center; and the Lonergan and Parrott families, especially Joe, Andrew and Emma.

CONTENTS

I

As God Would Have It

When you give us your word,
we take it the way a fisherman
rubs his hand down the spine

of a catch he knows he will
keep. We fold it like a map
to a secret lean-to in the woods.

Under the darkest branch of night,
you speak through silent dewfall,
liquefying complacent ice until it rises,

a vapor defining ascension.
We hover in the mist,
ready to rest in the cup of your hand,

that little ship of fingers waiting
to carry us away from the harbor
of our enemies, waiting to stoke
the epiphanic flame singeing within.

Lying in the Grass with Rumi

Translation of Coleman Barks'
Translation of "The Grasses" by Rumi

The wind knocks down trees easier than a man,
leaves the sun glowing on ravaged grass.

Kingship of the wind demands obedience,
a low bow from seagrass shows crowning strength.

A woodcutter doesn't consider thickness of trunk or limb.
He cuts it all, leaving stumps to mourn the leaves.

Fire pays no attention to the depth of the pit,
but a shepherd knows he must separate goats from sheep.

What is form in the presence of reality?

Is a cloudy sky
an inverted teacup?

Who tips the water jar
of heaven?

an inkling of faith

sometimes it's no more
than a flinch within,

a sacred leech worming the urge
to scratch below the skin of the soul.

quick as flutter, a flip turn
of a goldfish in a teacup,

you start to believe in strings
of oddities—a whale stomaching a man

before spitting him ashore alive,
a doubter dipping a curious finger

into a demitasse wound
like a fountain pen probing an inkwell

or a sea of red dividing itself easily
as a comb parting a slick head of hair.

Grasping the Hem of Divinity

Who touched My garments? –Mark 5:30

How long must I count myself
unclean? Seven days have bled
into seven hundred times seven.

By hand I dye and re-dye
my flaxen dress berry-red,
my removable red tent.

Stray dogs sniff me to the fringe
of a Mobius crowd roving
after a man fishing for men,

a man who can lift the bed sick,
a man who can carry himself,
a water jar divining its well.

Watchful mothers eye me
rubbing mustard balm in both
palms to mask the unspeakable

menstrual scent cloaking
the hocus of my body, the cloche
of flesh encasing the mystery of me.

Doulas, doctors and shamans
have emptied all remedies
bottled between their ears.

My right hand knows nothing is left.
I brave the breach of a forthright
reach into the spooler of threads.

Your Word

In the end you kept it
by giving it away
from the beginning.

From the beginning
your word was always there
waiting for us in silence.

Waiting for us in silence
your word watched as we
filled our jars with noise
omnipresent as sand.
Grain by grain it flowed
above our necks,
over our heads.

Over our heads
unable to be heard,
your word became a star
distracting our senses,
offering something undeserved,
something incarnate,
something called eternity.

Incarnate eternity
pierced a hole through
Bethlehem's sky,
radiating divinity
to the anticipated few
traveling slowly,
traveling surely
through sand,
through dromedary milieu.

Drawing Water

Fingertips of mist
disguise the buoyant gift,
a shallow creek
deep enough to ennoble
water's lowly flow
into submerged urns,
humble cups,
spoons of every depth:
demitasse, tea and table.

Woodland animals
don't know why
we carry water
against the sway,
against the heat
of our bodies,
the groan and grit
of hands belabored.

On nights like this
when the high-rise moon
won't let us sleep,
all the beasts
watch our reckless feet
rip into the water,
run wonder right through it,
shoes and all.

Drawing Children

Bless the dull
pencil tip

pressing letters
point by point

against ruled paper
guided by blue lines.

Bless the sharpener
restoring conical strength

to lead leading
design from mind to fingertip.

Bless the drawer
the drawing,
the drawn.

The Alpha, the Omega and the Tau

Repeat after me: (I tell the kindergarten girl)

A, B, C, D, E, F, G, H, I… (I wonder how long she will try)

J, K, L, M, N, O… (Oh, no one knows how much she knows)

P, Q, R, S, T… (*T* stops her)

I saw this letter before, she says, tapping her pencil against the paper.

She leaves the table to lie down face up in story-time corner.

I saw a man hanging on a big T. Like this. Who is he?

(I want to cant but can't: *He* is the *Alpha, Blessed, Christ, Deity,*
Emmanuel, Father, Good Shepherd, Heaven's Gate, Jesus, King of
Kings, Lamb of God, Messiah, Nazarene, Omega, Prince of Peace,
Quicquidlibet, Redeemer, Savior, Trinity, Universal Truth,
Virgin Mary's Son, Word of God, Xenagogue, Yeshua, Zion's Hope.)

He's "A" man named Jesus, I say, angling my arms into the letter *A.*

Oh!, she says, clasping her hands over her head, making the letter *O.*

Unknotting the Tie

Inspired by Jan Beatty

I scissor through blue construction paper
to make you a makeshift tie. I have run out
of real ones you left behind on the bus,
under your bed, on a playground somewhere.

You've got to make sure the kids are in uniform,
I hear the principal hiss in my head
as I rummage safety pins in my desk.

You never ask why I do this, unquestioning
as orphans who creep out of the books we read,
orphans who hide in secret gardens,

orphans who live in boxcars and are born
in the Bronx, destined to be gentrified.
They all live happily in their ever after.

You are the boy who never talks
about his mother, the boy who won't read
until you meet *Mr. Popper's Penguins*
and can't help but tell the whole class:

My mother used to have a pet alligator.
It walked through the house while she played
the piano, and we all sang, "She'll be coming 'round
the mountain, when she comes."

Pin Cushion

Stuffed with sawdust,
poked with wide-eyed
sewing needles, tin straight pins,
the little red tomato pillow
wobbles in my outstretched hand.
I fight the urge to ping
its tethered strawberry
while my seams are let out.

Don't move, scolds the PTA Mom.
My mind takes a walk in a pair
of Mary Janes, cranberry-red.
Two one-eyed Abes wink
from my penny loafers.

At school I sit in a row of my own,
train my eyes to keep each other
company as we travel the Silk Road
on a Rand McNally map.

The PTO mom stops smiling
when I can't fit in the expanded
oxen costume stitched for the holiday
play. "Silent Night" thrums in my head
as her dressmaker's tape snaps open and shut.

Independent Readers

Before the teacher reads
The Last of the Mohicans,

she announces this book marks
the last to be read aloud.

We wonder what sound
the turn of the final page will make.

Like budding botanists combing the woods
for treasures to squirrel away in a rucksack,

we collect her words: *Huron, Hawkeye,*
Narragansett, monsieur. We hold onto

Chingochgook, Natty Bumppo,
ears bent to the book.

Twigs snap. Pine sap clings
to evergreen needles blanketing

the forest floor. Fiery secrets
carried by young runners burn in our ears,

stone-headed arrows split the air,
chase lead bullets ablaze

while smoke burrows out
blackened rifle barrels.

War cries subside as we slip
into a cove of stillness by the banks

of the Mohawk. Darkness closes the lid
of day. We rest our heads in overgrown grass,

dreaming of the new path we will follow tomorrow,
without a trusty scout, without the compass of sound.

II

Tantrum Ergo

On a holy day to come they will say my mother loved
wearing wide-brimmed hats, elbow-length gloves—pretty stuff.
Scarves and shoes had to match. Pocketbook was queen.

Her favorite had a shimmy chain shoulder strap. Gold. Long
enough to crisscross her body. She was short. Father tall.
We all landed heights somewhere in between.

From me—and only me—she hid her purse. Chasing Chanel N°. 5,
I exhausted the house. She said she just couldn't take me
wherever a wallet or clutch bag was sold.

Pleather, leather, shiny vinyl, combed-cotton totes—I had to have them—
to hold something I didn't know how to carry. I zipped to unzip,
buckled to unbuckle. Flails and screams fled from me. And my mother?

She scooped me against her chest. Crimson cheeks skin to skin.
Unbuttoned my overheated store, carried me horizontally. I was
a briefcase, a satchel, a prickly little portmanteau dangling from her side.

Mother's Nature

In a tattered fishing hat, she collects pinecones,
stiff little round ones unable to lie flat. The lost,
the fallen, from trees Longleaf, Loblolly.

At home on the porch, she bashes
woody clusters with a lightweight hammer,
releasing sap, needles and seeds.

Soggy cones wobbly as wet cigars
get sacrificed twice, thrown over the fence
for a quick squirrel's breakfast.

With wind-burned hands she scatters
broken seedlings on a cardboard triangle,
cut isosceles for the making of a Christmas tree.

She gets bits of glitter to stick
with fixative spray, warns me
of the hazard of breathing it in.

Pert and yellow, a partridge tops
her holiday craft, and the whole thing hangs
by a thumbtack stuck in the front door.

Safe Storage

When dust freely takes over everything we keep, we clean.
Out of the attic, you carry a nativity I made years ago
for your plant stand. Clumsy green velvet takes the place
of sand, something new was coming home from Bethlehem.

Silver sequins glued to a rough-cut paper star
no longer muster shine, dull as raindrops captured in a jar.
Crisscrossed balsa wood legs hold up the infant bed,
layered with honey-colored shellac, pitted, scratched.

Shards of straw crumble at the thought of being touched,
and the hand-painted eyes of baby Jesus still don't close,
even now as I search His crib for the gift hardest
to give: a tiny button pierced with a rhinestone.

Mother Daughter Smoke Rings

Mother leaves
her cigarette at rest,
it burns the lip
of our kitchen sink.

Mother polishes
her fingernails
fire-engine red,
the ashen end
inches toward us.

Mother leaves
baby's bassinette,
cries of my sister
are cradled.

The crimson
flame within
self-extinguishes.

Pheasants

Grandma says it's no trouble to stay
for supper, but mother's eyes echo
emphatic *no*, adding twelve
to a table for four is too big for words.

Peeled Russet potatoes
bounce to a rolling boil in a deep pot
on the gas stove. I count spuds
to see if there's enough for all of us.

Grandma rolls pie dough on a wood block,
turning every stretch. Through a window
facing the maple-sugar shack, I count cows
dotting the hillside, clusters of black and white
checkers waiting to be moved.

I knock on grandfather's study door, the smell
of baked apples and lamb stays with me. My sisters
are inside, fighting over who gets to sit at his desk.
They flip through a calendar of Holstein photographs,
hoping to see something different each month.

Shoeless, I stand on a chair to look at a painting
of pheasants under glass. Tilting my head,
I see my face on a bird's wing.
I can't tell if we're running or flying.

In a Country Without Women

Men carry tranquilized birdseed in their pockets
for balance and the off chance of capturing—barehanded—
weensy animals that whoop, caw or squawk—to gut and stuff
in rucksacks, makeshift pillows. There are no beds.

In a smoky tavern, scrappy boys shadow box without music,
flail swollen fists in front of sweat-stained hunting jackets
hanging from cantilevered hooks above bootjacks
more pointed than the V-split of a king cobra's tongue.

Bituminous night paces the landscape. Insomniac bull frogs
snatch batches of mosquitoes, and all the cows are named after
heavy-weight prize fighters. And the crows? They peck
worm-eaten floorboards resurfaced more than the groin of midnight.

In a country without women, men speak body language with ease,
gesticulating arms, hands and feet—unhinging the shackles of speech.

Waltzing Through the Ramshackle Barn Dance

In Memory of Karl Parker

Not everybody wears pants. Some in fancy dress show their shins, and asking for a dance is easy as a bare-knuckle shoulder tap, but if you offer a touch more, you might just rile the backbone of a would-be partner's partner, ready to hand you a straight-arm shove through a horse stall. Cowboys can be fishermen. The fishiest pool in a corner nearest the door like land grabbers waiting for a starter-gun blast or a swig of whiskey from a flask etched with thirsty initials. The best hoofers swill beer. But when a tipsy liquor spill leads to a thunderclap on the jaw, drawing spittle and blood, the stout man with a megaphone and wrinkled mud on his boots shouts: *Bleeding's normal, folks. Bleeding's normal.*

The Upper Hand of Grendel's Mother

Slumpen men, sated by the gleam of swords loyal
to earthly burden of king and kin alike, why gyrate death
in this hollow den carved in the neck of a sunken cave?

Arise from wine-sacked sprawl of yeast wort and sticky mead,
blue cheese and horse sweat, iron smelt and fish skin
charred by fire-pit flames radiating gargantuan shadows.

You have no hunch I haunch within shouting distance,
wielding the firebrand of Cain to reclaim the remains
of what remains of my son. In his footpath I step to follow,
hell-bent on soldering the king to his own sword.

Guards are losing the sway between wake and sleep—
vulnerable as wanderlust sheep listing toward an open gate
on a moonless cliff. Through tangled vine and broken branch,
I sinew toward you, hapless as a bee smoked out a drowsy hive.

Listen. Heady snores beat the stick of vengeance against my
ear drum, pounding headache into heart ache. Alone I lay
in wait to lunge at the man who hangs my son's severed arm
—hand to shoulder—rafter high! See it dangle? See it drip?

Fathering the Son of the Father

From crown to brow,
mustache to chin,
sawdust rafts down
channels of sweat
mapped across your skin.

Taking hammer to chisel,
you pound to the *soto voce* beat,
a loom sliding in the hands
of your wife weaving
in the adjoining room.

In the folds of a handkerchief,
you seek more than a haven
for your eyes, you seek shade
dark enough to submerge submission
to a fatherhood from which you run.

God knows not many men
could wrestle the angel
of your dreams. And no man
but you could carve a cradle
from the belly of an unclaimed tree.

Under the Hood

She thinks I'm asleep in my oversized chair,
my daughter, tiptoeing with the bounce hop
she uses to dodge cracks in the sidewalk.

It's the same move that leaps her over my work
boots, the pair with serpentine laces that trip her
without warning, lightening without thunder.

Tonight the house rattles, she cannot sleep.
My hands become five-pointed stars combing night
light through her hair until her head leads her body

into the attic of dreams. Awake on my knees,
bent in prayer beside her bed, my good leg
buckles and shakes, an ancient column
breaking under the weight of its crown.

A Glimpse of Icarus at Webster's Pond

A rock shaped like the Island of Crete
rises above green water not deep enough
to make its own waves. It relies on geese
sailoring through stillness to ripple its surface.

Young birds preen on the pebbled shore,
giving lift to down mottling the air. A boy
the size of a swan runs toward them,
waving three long feathers in his small hand.
Don't you want these back? he asks.

Some birds plunge into the water,
others fly away. The boy's father
collects the feathers, lays them on a stone.
I pick up one and flutter it fast, then faster,
carried away by the beat of my own wings,
carried back to the final cry of my father.

Shadowing the Farmer

Over the double-pitched roof of the barn,
blue silos cast butter-knife shadows
across the John Deer at rest on your farm.

Unmilked cows stand in stalls, below
the half-stacked loft of hay, refuge of cats.
No rooster crows, the lone bull won't bellow.

Your pickup truck sits empty. Sunglasses
on the dash reflect a hint of daylight
beckoning confused chickens that ask

why the man who throws corn is not in sight.
They peck at stones no bigger than their eyes,
cluck for food, sensing something's not right.

Red hackle feathers tucked in their sides
bristle and flap as the birds try to rise
alongside the truck, though they cannot fly.

The wind refuses to lift their intentions,
the weathervane searches every direction.

Hunting the Afterlife

How can I sniff my way to heaven
with ice cream on my chin,
more fur than a *grand dame*
wears outside of winter?

You tell me to tell whoever is up there
it's all the groomer's fault
my unkempt coat rivals
the mange of Chewbacca.

You say she says I am too weak
for a sponge bath, hair-dryer heat.
Then you tell me to hang onto my leash
until I meet Saint Somebody,
like it's one big prayer chain up there.

And then— and then you ask me to *beg*
Saint Sebastian to lend a spare arrow
to comb my chenille Spaniel ears,
descending in my food bowl.
Aren't you coming with me?

Canine Lexicon

My dog wakes me
with a nudge of his nose
to tell me he wants to eat.
To eat, he wants to tell me.

His meals vary very little,
very little his meals vary.
Breakfast can be supper,
supper breakfast.

He shakes off the rain,
but the wind makes him shudder,
close both eyes like this.
I whistle 'til they open wide.

My dog walks beside me with ease,
with ease he walks beside me.
His lead is my leash,
my leash his lead.

Haiku

Bare trees in the woods
lean against one another,
sharing common ground.

Brave water still runs,
stands up against tough winter,
despite falling snow.

Duck prints in the snow
less than, greater than, equal
to the countless stones.

Five swans in a line
hiss as I inch near a sixth
awaiting a seventh.

Drops of rainwater
dangle under tree branches,
temporary pearls.

Maple leaves glide by
empty Adirondack chairs,
chasing after summer.

Seasoned Wood

Leaning over the empty crib, I lock it in place so it won't rock. Fall has come too late for gutters to fend off winter's brazen dress. Bonfire begs to be lit from kindling gathered from the failure of branches. If the wind promises to hold its breath, I'll loosen my scarf and listen low to the rattle keening off key in me.

War on the Domestic Front

Soldiers are chosen
by fortunes of straw,
only the boys draw
battle lines:
Germany is Mr. Mulhouser's yard
France, the Infantines' front porch,
the rest of the block belongs to the United States.

The girls are in the house making lemonade.

If you own a BB gun
you get to be a General.

The girls are in the house stirring lemonade.

Only girls sew
battle flags:
black, red and yellow German bands,
blue, blanc et rouge champs Français,
stars & stripes for the USA

The boys are at the kitchen window, begging baked goods.

Florence Nightingales
are chosen by a show
of bandages,
fingernails clean
as a baker's hands.

If you have a pocket
& can carry a secret,
you can be
Mata Hari with me.

The boys are in the kitchen, rummaging something white to wave.

Little Shoes After the Big War

Ekphrastic Reflection on a Photograph

With both arms you hug what's meant for your feet,
new brown shoes caught like two fish on the same
hook. They squirm and slide as you make a game
of holding them up, heels out, in the street.
Leather laces dangle like fishing lines
as you untangle them one at a time.

On stone steps you pause to take a quick rest,
rub your fingers across the top stitching
and over the curved toes, as if to test
how fast they will carry you home, running.
You sniff the shoes longer than a dog would
and laugh only as an unarmed boy could.

Rock Garden

I rake with the reach of a mother
endlessly tending leaves.

Hunched, squat, gloved,
I trowel the ground,

pry mounds of dirt, open mouths
unwilling to swallow.

Planting marigolds on my knees,
I wince against rogue stones

too big to lift or fit my fist, too heavy
to throw over the backyard fence.

I feel for pebbles and twigs,
tuck them under the skirt of a holly bush.

Rocks are harder to respect, except
the ones marking whereabouts of the dead.

In the Garden of You

Your garden has outlived you.
French lilacs speak your name
in soft pleas the way prisoners do.
Purple buds cluster like a crowd
of a thousand pinwheels, begging
the wind to carry their transcendent
scent across the apron strings of the sky.

Grounded in your flowerbed,
I kneel to the sun, wield a tool
tough enough to twist woody stems
unwilling to bend. I pound a hammer
against them until they splinter
into straw, forcing them to accept
transference from earth to container,
forcing them to continue to live.

Belief in the Making

God, why do you keep asking me to look for a ram in the battered thicket?
There are no brave animals here, no lambs, no turtle doves—nothing clean

to sacrifice. Every blemish hides a scar. You know what is under
my brambled skin, how many bruises nest on the heads of men

I toppled over benches, forsaken altars. Who can untangle this herd
huddled in the divide between public spaces and private entrances?

There are no rams to save us—Saul, Samuel, and Isaiah are dead.
Is there no other ear in which you can whisper? Mine still rings

from the night you sent an awkward bird to whistle my name.
Shrill funneled through a loose stitch in a pocket of the sky,

drilling so much rain I had to scramble like a man without a roof,
without an umbrella, with nothing but empty hands to press together

like bookends in prayer, as the onrush of rain pounded out a flood,
fishtailing my senses, and I flailed until all flailing failed to keep my soul

skeletal. God, how long can a man be reduced to full expansion,
slog through waterfall until he becomes spirited mist?

Water Ways

Double Triolet

Water seeks the lowest place,
digits of rivers, jawless mouth of the sea anemone,
splayed barbels on a catfish face.

Water seeks the highest place,
tsunami crown, arbiter of salinity of the sea,
eye sockets on a dying man's face.

Water seeks the lowest place,
terra-cotta urn bottom, basin of grace,
bent elbow of an estuary.

Water seeks the highest place
forehead of a newborn sanctified with grace,
the Holy Spirit's estuary.

Water seeks the lowest place
digits of rivers, jawless mouth of sea anemone.

Water seeks the highest place,
tsunami crown, arbiter of salinity of the sea.

About Sara Parrott

Sara Parrott's poetry has appeared in *Michigan Quarterly Review, Nine Mile Magazine, Stone Canoe, The Literary Nest, Dappled Things, Ghost City Review,* and *True Chili.* Several of her haiku are featured on posters created by the Syracuse Poster Project, including a commemorative poster celebrating the 50th-anniversary of Onondaga Community College in Syracuse, New York. She holds an MA from Binghamton University, and *Tipping the Water Jar of Heaven* is her first book.